Sauces and Dips

For Dazzling, Drizzling, and Dunking

> Authors: E. Döpp | C. Willrich | J. Rebbe

Contents

Appendix

Delicious Sauces and Luscious Dips: Irresistible!

Whether velvety smooth or fresh and tangy, a good sauce turns an already fine meal into pure pleasure. Whether you're looking for a beloved classic or a new recipe for experimentation—whether spicy, hearty, or sweet—you'll find a favorite sauce to satisfy every culinary whim. And if you're in a hurry, try one of the super-quick sauces at the beginning of each chapter.

Basic Recipe

Stocks and Broths

Almost every good sauce is based on a hearty stock or aromatic broth. Due to their neutral flavor profile, vegetable stocks (sometimes called court bouillon) are suitable for any sauce. But when you're serving fish, poultry, lamb, or beef, it's always better to prepare the corresponding stock for using in the sauce.

MAKES ABOUT
1 QUART STOCK:

➤ 4 lbs beef cut into pieces or 4 lbs finely chopped veal bones

1 onion

2 carrots

1/3 lb celery

1 leek

1 tbs oil

1 tbs tomato paste

2 cups red wine

1 bay leaf

2 sprigs each of thyme, marjoram, and parsley

Salt and pepper

TIP

Storing Stock

Let the stock cool, then skim the fat off the top. Freeze stock in usable-sized portions. For smaller amounts, use ice-cube trays, and then store the cubes of stock in freezer bags.

> **1** Rinse and dry meat or bones. Peel onion. Rinse and peel/trim vegetables. Cut everything into coarse pieces. Preheat oven to 350°F.

> **2** In a very large ovenproof pot, pan, or dutch oven (use multiple pans if necessary), heat oil and brown meat or bones over high heat. Add vegetables and brown. Stir in tomato paste.

> **3** Pour in wine and 4 cups water. Add bay leaf and other herbs and bring to a boil. Place in the oven (middle rack), let simmer there for 2 hours, then pour through a strainer, discarding the solids.

Stock Variations

To obtain a truly aromatic stock, you have to "reduce it." You'll be amazed how much this intensifies the flavor. Reducing is achieved by long simmering times. The pros often simmer their stock so long that it takes on a thick, syrupy consistency. This kind of stock is called a "glace" or "demi glace" and gives meat sauces fantastic flavor. You can freeze this reduced stock in ice-cube trays; otherwise it will keep in the refrigerator for at least a week.

Gravy is achieved by preparing a large roast with roasted onions and vegetables and then thickening the pan juices. In this case you don't necessarily need to add stock to those juices, but it can't hurt, and will make the gravy even better.

Chicken Stock

Chicken stock is popular but you can also use other types of poultry. To make an aromatic stock, follow the recipe for meat stock on page 4 but instead of meat bones use 4 lbs finely chopped chicken parts with the bones (necks, wings, backs).

Lamb and Game Stock

Prepare basic stock recipe (page 4) using 4 lbs lamb or game bones with a little meat but instead of marjoram, use rosemary and sauté 2 unpeeled garlic cloves with the meat.

Fish Stock

Bring 1 quart water to a boil with 2 lbs fish bones (ask your fish-monger), 1 bay leaf, 1 sprig thyme, and $1/2$ lb chopped vegetables (celery, carrots, onion, leek, etc.) and simmer uncovered for 20–30 minutes. Strain, discarding the solids.

Vegetable Stock

In 1 quart water, simmer $1/2$ pound grated carrots, $1/4$ pound rinsed and minced leek, $1/2$ onion (grated), $1/4$ lb minced celery, 1 bay leaf, 1 pinch freshly grated nutmeg, 1 tsp turmeric powder, pepper, and salt for 15 minutes. Strain, discarding the solids.

The Basics of Thickening Sauces

Thickening, or binding, is a technique often used to turn a good sauce into a delicacy. Various options exist, including using starch, eggs, cream, and butter.

1 | Thickening with Starch

Thicken 1 cup sauce liquid with:

- 1 tbs cornstarch, flour, or potato starch. Stir cornstarch into 3 tbs cold water. Then stir into hot sauce liquid (removed from the heat source). Return to heat and bring to a boil. Cornstarch binds immediately, even before the sauce reaches 200°F.

Thickening: Stir starch into water and then into the heated sauce.

- 1 tsp carob flour (available in health food stores and supermarkets), which you can stir directly into the hot sauce. Then bring the sauce to a boil. The advantage of carob flour is that you don't have to stir it into water first but can add it directly to the sauce as an instant binder.
- 2 to 3 oz grated potatoes that you boil separately for 4 minutes, then purée and finally stir into the sauce as a thickener.

2 | Binding with Egg Yolk

For 1 cup sauce liquid, whisk together 2 egg yolks and ¼ cup of the sauce liquid; stir this mixture back into the hot sauce (removed from the heat); return to a low heat to slowly reduce the sauce, but don't let it boil.

3 | Binding with Cream

Stir ⅔ cup cream into 1½ cups sauce liquid. Bring to a boil and reduce sauce by half to thicken.

Binding of the pros: Cut ice-cold butter into bits and stir into the sauce, little by little.

Or add ½ cup crème fraîche to 1⅔ cups sauce liquid and slowly reduce by half.

4 | Binding with Butter

Cut 3 tbs ice-cold butter into bits and stir into sauce, little by little, while swirling the pan. Kneaded butter, which is a mixture of starch or flour and butter, is another good option for binding sauces. Knead together 1 tsp flour and 1 tsp butter into a ball and stir into the sauce with a wire whisk. Pros call this kneaded butter "beurre manié."

Little Helpers

Prepared sauce mixes (see page 8): Today every supermarket offers jars and packets of sauces. If you feel timid in the kitchen, use them to jazz up your own sauce or buy one and enhance it yourself with flavorful additions.

Broths and stocks: Dried stocks and bouillons are very practical as a way to add seasoning. A wide range of prepared stocks are available in powders, cubes, jars, cans, and frozen tubs including meat, poultry, game, fish/ seafood, and sometimes even mushroom. Check specialty stores.

Herbs: Fresh herbs give sauces finesse and character. But don't add the herbs to the sauce too early or they'll lose a lot of their aroma and pungency. It's best to stir them into the sauce just before serving, then let the sauce rest for 1 minute.

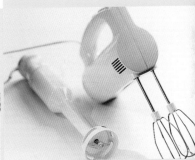

Spiced oils: For rosemary oil, stir $1/2$ tsp rosemary needles, $1/2$ clove garlic and 1 tsp fresh lemon juice into heated oil. For garlic chile oil, stir toasted slices of 1 garlic clove and $1/2$ chile pepper into unheated oil. Great for drizzling.

Wire whisks: Various types of whisks are available for stirring and beating sauces. They include twirl, French, spiral, and flat styles, as well as the traditional whisk (such as what is used to whisk eggs) — a must-have for your kitchen.

Hand blender and mixer: A powerful hand blender is ideal for binding the separate components of a sauce. Beating in butter or cream gives sauces a desirable foaminess.

7

Pepping Up Prepared Sauces

White sauces:

A white sauce is a basic for casseroles, vegetable dishes, cooked fish, meat, and poultry (check for cans, packets, and jars in the supermarket.)

Mustard sauce: Season white sauce with 1 tsp mustard, 1–2 tbs crème fraîche, salt, and pepper.

Gorgonzola sauce: Chop 2 shallots and ¹⁄₂ clove garlic and sauté in 2 tsp butter until translucent. Add 3¹⁄₂ oz Gorgonzola, 2 tbs crème fraîche, and 1 cup heated white sauce. Mix with a hand blender until smooth. Season to taste with salt, pepper, and fresh lemon juice.

Horseradish sauce: Season white sauce with 3 tbs horseradish, fresh lemon juice, and a little cream.

Gravies:

If you don't have enough pan juices from your steak or if you want more gravy with your Sunday roast than was produced by the meat, it's time to use a pre-made gravy (check for cans, packets, and jars in the supermarket).

Cream gravy: Add enough broth or stock to the pan juices to make 1 cup. Prepare gravy according to package directions if using a packet. Add to pan liquids, heat, and thicken with starch (see page 6). Refine with 2 tbs cream or crème fraîche before serving.

Garlic gravy: Briefly sauté 2 finely chopped garlic cloves in 2 tsp oil. Chop 1 tomato and sauté with garlic. Add 1 tbs red wine and bring to a boil. Stir in 1 cup pre-made gravy (that has been heated through). Pour through a strainer, bring to a boil, and stir in 1 tbs butter cut into bits. Mix with a hand blender.

Hollandaise sauce:

Simply unbeatable with asparagus and salmon, and thanks to finished products, you no longer have to shy away from making this egg and butter sauce (check for cans, packets, and jars in the supermarket.)

Maltaise sauce: Season hollandaise sauce to taste with 2 tbs blood orange juice and 1 tbs grated orange peel.

Mousseline sauce: Stir 3 tbs whipped cream into warm hollandaise sauce and season to taste with paprika and 1 pinch cayenne pepper.

Lemon sauce: Mix sauce with 2 tsp grated lemon peel and season to taste with fresh lemon juice.

Tomato sauce:

This Italian classic goes great with all types of pasta. Be sure to purchase high-quality sau (the fewer the additive the better). Check for cans and jars in the supermarket.

Tomato olive sauce: Stir 4–8 chopped black olives and 1–2 tbs cap into the sauce.

Tomato fennel sauce: Sauté ¹⁄₃ lb diced fenn 1 chopped garlic clove and 1 chopped onion translucent. Add 1 dice tomato and simmer fo 5 minutes; add tomato sauce and season with salt and pepper.

Tomato Mascarpone sauce: Stir mascarpon into the sauce until it appears creamy, add salt and pepper, and fi ish it off with fresh bas

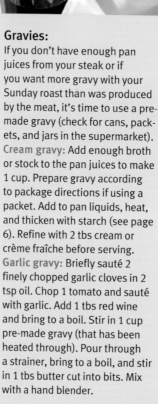

Troubleshooting—What To Do If...

The sauce is lumpy

➤ Beat the sauce vigorously with a hand blender or pour it through a strainer.

The sauce has burned onto the pan

➤ Stop stirring so you won't spread the bitter taste through the sauce. Pour the sauce into a fresh pot and reheat while stirring. While the other soiled pan is still hot, add water and try to scrape up the burned bits, quickly, to ease later clean-up. Let the soiled pan soak.

The sauce is too spicy

➤ Simply add a little broth, stock, cream, or water, as desired.

The sauce is too salty

➤ Peel and rinse a potato, cut into pieces, and simmer in the sauce.

The sauce is too runny

➤ Reduce the sauce and finish it off by beating in 1–2 tbs ice-cold butter in bits or kneaded butter (beurre manié) using a wire whisk. Then beat sauce once again briefly with a hand blender. Or, even easier, mix some corn starch with a little cold water and add to the sauce; return sauce to a gentle boil until thickened.

The sauce is too thick

➤ Add a little more liquid and blend the sauce with a hand blender. If you want, you can stir a little whipped cream into the sauce and serve immediately.

The mayonnaise is too thick

➤ Carefully fold in a little beaten egg white or yogurt, but do not stir vigorously. This will make the mayonnaise fluffier.

The hollandaise sauce has curdled

➤ Immediately remove the pot from the water bath and using a hand blender, blend in 1 ice cube, 1 tbs ice water or ice-cold cream. Or start over with a fresh egg yolk and use the curdled sauce in place of the melted butter from the original recipe (see page 17).

The mayonnaise has curdled

➤ Start over with 1 fresh egg yolk (at room temperature, not straight out of the refrigerator!). Add and stir in curdled mayonnaise one drop at a time.

Classics

There's no doubt about it—the basis for all good cooking is the sauce. And no sauce-lover can do without the classics! Hollandaise sauce beaten until creamy and served with asparagus never goes out of style.

Quick Recipes

Vegetable Sauce

SERVES 4:

➤ 1 potato | 1 cup vegetable stock |
²/₃ lb mixed vegetables (carrots, leek,
mushrooms) | 1 tbs olive oil | 1 cup milk |
1 tbs chopped fresh parsley |
1 pinch nutmeg | Salt and pepper |
2 tbs fresh lemon juice

1 | Peel potato, rinse, grate coarsely, and
cook in ½ cup of the stock for 3 minutes,
then purée.

2 | Rinse vegetables well (especially leeks)
and cut into matchstick strips. Heat olive oil
and sauté vegetables until translucent. Add
milk and remaining stock and heat; then
simmer for 4 minutes. Add potato purée and
parsley and season to taste with nutmeg, salt,
pepper, and fresh lemon juice.

➤ Serve with: Pasta, meats, fish, vegetables

Bell Pepper Sauce

SERVES 4:

➤ 3 red and yellow bell peppers | 4 green
onions | 1 tbs olive oil | 2 cups vege-
table stock | Salt and pepper | 2 tbs
crème fraîche

1 | Rinse bell peppers and green onions
and chop usable parts of both.

2 | Heat olive oil and sauté onions and
peppers until translucent. Add stock and
heat; simmer for 15 minutes. Purée sauce
with a hand blender, season with salt and
pepper, and stir in crème fraîche to finish.

➤ Serve with: Pasta, chicken, quiche,
roasted or grilled vegetables

11

Can Prepare in Advance | Fast

Béchamel Sauce

SERVES 4:

➤ 1½ cups milk
  3 tbs butter
  2 tbs flour
  Salt and pepper
  1 pinch nutmeg

🕙 Prep time: 20 minutes
➤ Calories per serving: About 135

1 | Heat milk in a small pan. (If you want to get fancy, heat it up with 1 whole clove stuck into ½ an onion; remove clove and onion before using milk.)

2 | In a second pot, melt butter, add flour, and heat for 5 minutes while stirring constantly until the flour changes appearance slightly to a pale golden color.

3 | Gradually add hot milk while stirring constantly with a wire whisk. Bring to a boil while stirring constantly. Then simmer gently over low heat for 10 minutes, stirring

frequently. Season sauce to taste with salt, pepper, and nutmeg.

➤ Serve with: Sautéed fish, chicken, cauliflower, kohlrabi, peas with mint, potatoes, other cooked vegetables, and in or on top of baked casseroles

Fast | Hearty

Herbed Cheese Topping

SERVES 4:

➤ ¼ cup flour
  ¾ cup fresh basil sprigs
  1 onion
  1 tbs oil
  1½ cups milk
  Salt and pepper
  Freshly grated nutmeg
  ¼ cup freshly grated Parmesan
  1 egg yolk

🕙 Prep time: 15 minutes
➤ Calories per serving: About 180

1 | Heat flour in a pan until golden and then let cool. Rinse basil, remove leaves from stems, and mince. Peel onion and chop finely.

2 | In a pot, heat oil and sauté onion until translucent. Remove pot from heat. Add milk and flour and beat sauce with a hand blender. Return to heat and bring to a boil while stirring constantly. Then simmer gently over low heat for 5 minutes, stirring frequently. Season to taste with salt, pepper, nutmeg, basil, and Parmesan.

3 | In a cup, whisk together egg yolk and a little of the sauce and stir this mixture back into the sauce 1 tbs at a time. Don't let the sauce boil or it will curdle.

➤ Can be baked into or on top of casseroles, on top of vegetables and fish, and as a sauce with tortellini, gnocchi, cooked celery or broccoli, or other vegetables

Photo top: Béchamel Sauce   *Photo bottom:* **Herbed Cheese Topping** ➤

Hearty | Easy
Ground Meat Sauce

SERVES 4:
➤ 1 carrot
   1/4 pound celery root
   1 onion
   4 ripe fresh tomatoes
   2 tsp olive oil
   1 lb ground meat
   Salt and pepper
   2 tbs tomato paste
   1/4 cup vegetable stock

🕐 Prep time: 45 minutes
➤ Calories per serving: About 305

1 | Rinse carrots and celery root; peel and dice both finely. Peel onion and dice finely. Rinse tomatoes and chop.

2 | In a pot, heat oil and sauté carrots, celery root, and onion until onion is translucent. Add ground meat and brown until crumbly. Season with salt and pepper. Add tomato paste and tomatoes. Pour in stock and simmer sauce, covered, for 30 minutes.

➤ Serve with: Pasta, vegetables

Asian |Fast
Sweet-and-Sour Sauce

SERVES 4:
➤ 1/2 red bell pepper
   1 onion
   1 piece fresh ginger (1-inch section)
   1 tbs garlic-chile oil (see page 7)
   2/3 cup vegetable stock
   3 tbs ketchup
   2 tbs sugar
   1/3 cup rice vinegar
   2 1/2 tbs cornstarch
   Salt

🕐 Prep time: 15 minutes
➤ Calories per serving: About 85

1 | Rinse bell pepper and discard unusable parts. Peel onion. Dice both finely. Peel and grate ginger.

2 | Heat oil and sauté onion and bell pepper until translucent. Add stock, ketchup, sugar, rice vinegar, and ginger; bring to a boil. Stir cornstarch into 1/4 cup cold water. Stir mixture into sauce, bring to a boil, and season to taste with salt.

➤ Serve with: Asian dishes

Mediterranean | For Company
Parmesan Sauce

SERVES 4:
➤ 1 small onion
   2 tsp oil
   1/4 cup white wine
   1 cup vegetable stock
   1 tbs cornstarch
   1 sprig fresh thyme
   2 bay leaves
   2/3 cup sour cream
   5 oz freshly grated Parmesan
   Salt and pepper

🕐 Prep time: 10 minutes
➤ Calories per serving: About 250

1 | Peel and dice onion. Heat oil and sauté onion until translucent. Add wine and vegetable stock; bring to a boil. Stir cornstarch into 3 tbs cold water and add; stir until thickened. Add thyme and bay leaf and reduce sauce by one-third its volume.

2 | Remove thyme and bay leaf. Using a hand blender, blend sour cream into sauce; heat but do not boil. Just before serving, stir in Parmesan and salt and pepper to taste.

➤ Serve with: Pasta, poultry, vegetables

For Company | Impressive

Hollandaise Sauce

SERVES 4:

- ➤ 4½ oz butter (1 stick + 1 tbs)
- 2 egg yolks
- 2 tbs vegetable stock or water
- 1 tbs fresh lemon juice
- 1 pinch chili powder (optional)
- Salt and pepper

⏱ Prep time: 20 minutes
➤ Calories per serving: About 280

1 | In a pot, melt butter over medium heat. Remove from heat and let white part (the whey) sink to the bottom, a process known as "clarifying." Carefully skim off butter and keep warm in another pot.

2 | In a stainless steel bowl, whisk together egg yolks, stock, and fresh lemon juice. Place bowl over a hot (but not boiling) water bath (about 1 inch simmering water in the bottom of a pot) so it rests snugly and beat egg yolks with a wire whisk until they form a thick and creamy mixture.

3 | Remove bowl from water bath and using a wire whisk, gradually beat clarified butter into egg mixture, first drop by drop and then in a thin stream. If the sauce is too thick when you're done, add a little stock.

4 | If desired, season to taste with chili powder, salt, and pepper; serve at once.

➤ Serve with: Any fine vegetable dishes but traditionally with asparagus. Also tastes great with steak, chicken, poached trout, and salmon.

TIP

For a successful sauce, use a water bath so you can regulate the temperature more easily. (If the sauce gets too cold, it won't become creamy; if it gets too hot, it will curdle.) Use very fresh eggs, preferably free-range. The fresher the egg yolk, the more easily it will bind with the butter.

1 Clarify butter
Melt butter in a pot, discarding the white solids.

2 Whisk egg yolks
Whisk egg yolks with stock and lemon juice.

3 Beat egg yolks
Beat egg yolks until creamy.

4 Beat in butter
Off the heat, whisk in clarified butter.

Hearty | Low-Fat

Horseradish Sauce

SERVES 4:

- 1 onion
  2 tbs flour
  $1/2$ cup milk
  1 tsp oil
  $1/2$ cup white wine (or stock)
  3 tbs prepared horseradish
  1 tbs fresh lemon juice
  Salt and pepper

- Prep time: 20 minutes
- Calories per serving: About 55

1 | Peel onion and chop very finely. In a small bowl, whisk flour into milk.

2 | Heat oil and sauté onion until translucent. Add white wine and reduce by one-third. Stir in milk mixture and simmer uncovered for 3 minutes. Season sauce to taste with horseradish, fresh lemon juice, salt, and pepper.

- **Serve with: Stewed vegetables, celery, poached meats or fish, steaks, savory crepes**

For Company | Easy

Shallot and Red Wine Sauce

SERVES 4:

- 3 shallots
  1 tbs butter
  1 tbs honey
  1 sprig rosemary
  $1/3$ cup red wine
  1 tbs balsamic vinegar
  $1 1/4$ cups poultry stock
  1 tbs cornstarch
  Salt and pepper

- Prep time: 15 minutes
- Calories per serving: About 120

1 | Peel shallots and cut into strips. In a pan, cook butter and honey until golden (medium heat); add and sauté shallots and rosemary until translucent. Add wine and balsamic vinegar and heat, then simmer for 1 minute. Add stock, bring to a boil, and simmer until sauce is reduced by one-third.

2 | Stir cornstarch into 2 tbs cold water and stir into simmering sauce. Heat, then add salt and pepper to taste.

- **Serve with: Meat, fish, poultry**

Special Occasions | Fast

Mushroom Sauce

SERVES 4:

- $1/2$ lb shiitake mushrooms (or white, cremini)
  3 green onions
  2 tsp olive oil
  $1/3$ cup port wine (optional)
  $1 1/4$ cups poultry stock
  Salt and pepper
  1 tsp cornstarch

- Prep time: 20 minutes
- Calories per serving: About 105

1 | Rinse mushrooms and onions. Halve or quarter mushrooms. Chop onions.

2 | Heat olive oil and sauté mushrooms and white part of onions (reserve greens). Add port wine and stock; simmer until reduced by one-third. Stir cornstarch into a little cold water. Add to sauce and heat; season sauce with salt and pepper. Stir in onion greens before serving.

- **Serve with: Ribbon pasta, steak, chicken, quiche, casseroles**

Warm Sauces

For gourmets of all types, here are sauces "to die for." These favorites are ideal accompaniments for pasta, rice, and potatoes, and are fantastic complements to fish, meat, and poultry—the hit of any barbecue.

Quick Recipes

Curry Leek Sauce

SERVES 4:

➤ $^1/_4$ lb leeks | 1 onion | 1 apple | 3 tsp curry powder | 2 tsp oil | 1 cup vegetable stock | $^1/_3$ cup cream | $^1/_4$ cup whole milk cottage cheese | 3 tbs fresh lemon juice | Salt and pepper

1 | Rinse leeks, onion, and apple—peel and chop all three finely.

2 | In a pot, heat curry and oil and sauté leeks, onion, and apple until tender. Add stock, heat, and keep cooking to reduce sauce slightly.

3 | Add cream and simmer for 5 minutes. Add cottage cheese and purée all with a hand blender. Finally, add fresh lemon juice and season to taste with salt and pepper.

➤ **Serve with: Fish (e.g., cod or halibut), rabbit, chicken breast**

Fresh Tomato Sauce

SERVES 4:

➤ 1 onion | 1 clove garlic | 2 oz celeriac (celery root) | $^1/_4$ lb carrots | $^1/_2$ lb tomatoes | 2 tsp olive oil | 1 sprig thyme | 1 bay leaf | Salt and pepper

1 | Peel and dice onion and garlic. Rinse and peel celeriac and carrots, and rinse tomatoes; then dice all finely.

2 | Heat oil and sauté onion and garlic until translucent. Add celeriac, carrots, and tomatoes; cook for 4 minutes. Add thyme and bay leaf. Simmer sauce for 6 more minutes. Season to taste with salt and pepper. Remove thyme and bay leaf before serving.

➤ **Serve with: Pasta, steak, tuna, braised fish, gnocchi, zucchini, Greek moussaka, grilled vegetables**

Can Prepare in Advance |
Mediterranean

Tomato Sauce with Capers and Tuna

SERVES 4:

➤ 2 small red onions
   1/2 lb fresh ripe tomatoes
   2 tsp olive oil
   1 tsp fresh thyme
   (may substitute dried)
   1 bay leaf
   1 pinch marjoram
   2 anchovy fillets
   2 tbs capers (rinsed)
   3 1/2 oz water-packed tuna
   Salt and pepper

🕐 Prep time: 30 minutes
➤ Calories per serving:
   About 110

1 | Peel red onions and chop finely. Rinse tomatoes, dice finely, and purée coarsely using a food processor, blender, or with a hand blender.

2 | In a pot, heat 1 tsp of the olive oil and sauté half the red onion over medium heat until translucent. Add tomato purée, thyme, and bay leaf; heat and then simmer sauce over low heat for 8 minutes.

3 | While the sauce simmers, heat remaining oil in another pot and sauté remaining onions over medium heat until translucent. Stir in marjoram and anchovies. After 3 minutes, mash anchovies slightly. Add finished tomato sauce and bring to a boil. Add capers and tuna and simmer over low heat. Season sauce to taste with salt and pepper.

➤ Serve with: Penne or other pasta, stewed or grilled vegetables, fried or sautéed fish, rabbit

Spicy | Can Prepare
in Advance

Tomato-Eggplant Sauce

SERVES 4:

➤ 2 red onions
   2 cloves garlic
   1/2 lb ripe fresh tomatoes
   2 tbs olive oil
   1 tsp chopped fresh oregano leaves
   2 bay leaves
   Salt and pepper
   1 eggplant (a little over 1/2 lb)
   1/2 fresh chile pepper (jalapeño or serrano)

🕐 Prep time: 30 minutes
➤ Calories per serving:
   About 75

1 | Peel onions and garlic and chop both finely. Rinse tomatoes, dice, and purée coarsely in a food processor, blender, or with a hand blender.

2 | Heat 1 tsp of the olive oil and sauté onions until translucent. Add garlic, tomatoes, oregano, and bay leaves; heat then simmer sauce for 8 minutes over low heat. Season with salt and pepper.

3 | Rinse eggplant and dice (minus stem). Chop chile pepper (first remove stem and seeds). In a second pan, heat remaining olive oil and brown eggplant and chile pepper. Add tomato sauce mixture. Bring to a boil and then reduce heat and simmer for 15 minutes. Season with salt and pepper. (Remove bay leaves before serving.)

➤ Serve with: Any type of pasta, fried or sautéed fish, stewed potato dishes, lasagna, couscous, and brown rice

Vegetarian | Low-Fat

Asian Vegetable Sauce

SERVES 4:

- ➤ 1 onion
  1 piece fresh ginger
  (1-inch section)
  2 carrots
  1 zucchini
  2 tsp garlic chile oil
  (see page 7)
  $1/3$ cup soy sauce
  $1/2$ cup vegetable stock
  $1/4$ lb bean sprouts
  Salt and pepper

- ⏱ Prep time: 20 minutes
- ➤ Calories per serving:
  About 155

TIP

You can, of course, replace the homemade spiced oil with any neutral oil (e.g., canola). But in that case, add 1 finely chopped garlic clove and $1/2$ chopped chile pepper to the sauce, preferably at the same time you add the onion.

1 | Peel onion, ginger, and carrots. Rinse zucchini and trim away ends. Mince ginger. Dice onion, carrots and zucchini into $1/2$-inch cubes.

2 | In a pot, heat oil over medium heat and sauté onion and carrots for 2 minutes. Add ginger and cook for 1 minute; then add soy sauce and stock.

3 | Rinse bean sprouts, drain, and add along with zucchini to sauce. Simmer for another 2 minutes. Season to taste with salt and pepper.

- ➤ Serve with: Rice, Chinese noodles, whole-grain spaghetti, fried or sautéed fish, poultry

For Company | Asian

Clam Sauce

SERVES 4:

- ➤ 2 lbs clams
  1 clove garlic
  1 small carrot
  $1/2$ small leek
  1 piece fresh ginger
  (1-inch section)
  1 tsp olive oil
  $3^1/2$ tbs white wine
  $1/3$ cup vegetable stock
  $1/3$ cup cream
  Salt and pepper
  3 tbs chopped fresh parsley

- ⏱ Prep time: 30 minutes
- ➤ Calories per serving:
  About 135

1 | Rinse and scrub clams (discard any that remain open). Rinse garlic, carrot, and leek; peel and chop all three finely. Peel ginger and grate finely.

2 | In a pot, heat olive oil and sauté garlic along with carrot and leek until leek is translucent. Add wine and stock and bring to a boil. Reduce heat, add cream, and simmer for another 5 minutes.

3 | Add clams and simmer for 5–8 minutes. (Discard any clams that stay closed.) Season with grated ginger, salt, pepper, and parsley.

- ➤ Serve with: Rigatoni, penne, or other pasta; vegetable risotto, grilled or sautéed fish

Hearty | Low-Fat

Onion-Marjoram Sauce

SERVES 4:
- ½ lb onions
  1 tbs oil
  1 cup vegetable stock
  1 tbs soy sauce
  1 tbs chopped fresh marjoram
  1 tbs cornstarch
  Salt and pepper

⏱ Prep time: 30 minutes
- Calories per serving: About 60

1 | Peel onions and dice finely. In a pot, heat oil and sauté onions over medium heat until translucent. Add stock and bring to a boil. Season with soy sauce and marjoram.

2 | Stir cornstarch into a little cold water and stir into simmering sauce using a wire whisk. Heat and then season to taste with salt and pepper.

- **Serve with:** Zucchini, carrots, fried or sautéed chicken or turkey, roast pork, veggie burgers

For Company | Easy

Prosecco Sauce

SERVES 4:
- 2 shallots
  3 tbs flour
  ½ cup cream
  1 tsp oil
  1 cup Prosecco (sparkling Italian white wine)
  1 tbs mixed chopped fresh herbs (e.g., chervil, chives, marjoram)
  Salt and pepper

⏱ Prep time: 15 minutes
- Calories per serving: About 170

1 | Peel shallots and mince. Whisk flour into cream.

2 | In a pot, heat oil and sauté shallots over medium heat until translucent. Add Prosecco and bring to a boil, then simmer for 3 minutes. Add flour-cream mixture while stirring, along with herbs, and simmer sauce for another 3 minutes. Season to taste with salt and pepper.

- **Serve with:** Turbot, whitefish, salmon, rabbit, vegetable dishes

Fast | Impressive

Cranberry-Chestnut Sauce

SERVES 4:
- 1 red onion
  2 bay leaves
  1 whole clove
  2 juniper berries
  1 cup cranberries
  ⅔ cup chestnuts (peeled)
  1 tbs butter
  1 tbs honey
  ⅓ cup white wine
  1¼ cups poultry stock
  Salt and pepper

⏱ Prep time: 20 minutes
- Calories per serving: About 160

1 | Peel and dice onion. Crush bay leaf, whole clove, and juniper berries; place in a tea ball. Rinse cranberries. Chop chestnuts.

2 | Sauté onion in butter until translucent. Add honey and cranberries; allow to caramelize while continuing cooking. Add wine, stock, and tea ball; simmer for 8 minutes. Purée sauce coarsely using a hand blender, and add chestnuts, salt, and pepper.

- **Serve with:** Game, turkey, cabbage dishes

Mediterranean | For Company
Rabbit Sauce with Olives

SERVES 4:

- ➤ 12 oz rabbit (leg meat; have butcher remove bones)
- 2 large ripe tomatoes
- 2 stalks celery
- 1 carrot
- 1 red onion
- 2 cloves garlic
- 1 sprig fresh rosemary
- 10 black kalamata olives
- 1 tbs olive oil
- $\frac{1}{2}$ cup white wine
- 1 cup poultry stock (homemade or canned)
- 1 tbs cornstarch
- Salt and pepper
- 1–2 tbs balsamic vinegar (optional)

⏲ Prep time: 1 hour

➤ Calories per serving: About 350

1 | Cut rabbit meat into small cubes. Rinse vegetables. Dice tomato finely. Cut celery into $\frac{1}{2}$-inch thick slices. Peel carrot and dice finely. Peel and dice onion; peel and mince garlic. Rinse rosemary. Remove pits from olives (or purchase pre-pitted variety).

2 | In a pot, heat oil and sauté rabbit cubes over medium heat until golden-brown.

3 | Lightly sauté celery, carrot, and onion. Next sauté tomatoes. Add garlic and rosemary and cook for another 5 minutes.

4 | Add wine and stock and heat; let simmer on low heat for about 30 minutes.

5 | Remove rosemary sprig. Stir cornstarch into 3 tbs cold water and add that mixture to simmering sauce. Stir in olives and simmer sauce for 4 minutes. Season to taste with salt and pepper, and with balsamic vinegar if desired.

➤ **Serve with:** Pasta such as rigatoni or penne; gnocchi, spaetzle, or mashed potatoes

1 Brown
Sauté diced rabbit until golden-brown.

2 Sauté the vegetables
Sauté vegetables while stirring.

3 Add liquid
Pour in wine and stock.

4 Thicken
Bind sauce with a cornstarch-water mixture.

29

Easy | For Company

Walnut Sauce

SERVES 4:

➤ 2 shallots
   $1/2$ cup walnuts
   1 tbs walnut oil
   $2/3$ cup vegetable stock
   $2/3$ cup meat stock
   (homemade or canned)
   1 tsp thyme
   Salt and pepper
   1 tbs cornstarch

🕐 Prep time: 20 minutes
➤ Calories per serving:
   About 135

1 | Peel shallots and mince. Chop walnuts.

2 | In a pot, heat oil and sauté minced shallots over medium heat for 1 minute until translucent. Add walnuts and cook for 1 minute.

3 | Add vegetable and meat stocks and bring to a boil. Next, reduce heat and simmer over low heat for 3 minutes. Season to taste with thyme, salt, and pepper.

4 | Stir cornstarch into $1/4$ cup cold water and add to the sauce to thicken it.

➤ **Serve with: Sautéed or roasted poultry, rabbit, and game**

Exotic | Fast

Passion Fruit Sauce

SERVES 4:

➤ 2 shallots
   4 passion fruit
   2 tsp oil
   1 cup poultry stock
   (homemade or canned)
   2 tbs soy sauce
   Salt and pepper
   1 pinch nutmeg
   1 tsp cornstarch

🕐 Prep time: 20 minutes
➤ Calories per serving:
   About 100

1 | Peel shallots and mince. Cut passion fruit in half, remove interiors, and place in a bowl.

2 | In a pot, heat oil and sauté minced shallots over medium heat for 1 minute until translucent.

3 | Add poultry stock. Bring sauce to a boil and then simmer over low heat for 3 minutes.

4 | Add soy sauce and season with salt, pepper, and nutmeg.

5 | Stir cornstarch into a little cold water and stir into sauce using a wire whisk. Stir in passion fruit. Let heat until slightly thickened—ready to serve.

➤ **Serve with: Sautéed fish, roast duck, turkey, seafood**

For Company | Easy

Orange-Basil Sauce

SERVES 4:

➤ 2 shallots

 1 orange

 1 tsp olive oil

 $1/3$ cup freshly squeezed orange juice (from 1 orange)

 $1/2$ cup dry white wine

 1 cup vegetable stock

 2 tbs chopped basil

 Salt and pepper

 1 tbs cornstarch

 $1/2$ cup sour cream

 8–12 whole basil leaves

🕐 Prep time: 30 minutes

➤ Calories per serving: About 100

1 | Peel shallots and chop finely. Zest about $1/4$ of the orange. Peel orange and separate into segments.

2 | In a pot, heat oil and sauté shallots until translucent. Add juice, wine, and stock; simmer for 8 minutes to reduce sauce by one-third its volume. Add chopped basil and simmer for 5 minutes. Season sauce to taste with salt and pepper.

3 | Stir cornstarch into a little cold water and then stir into simmering sauce to thicken; heat. Put sauce through a strainer. Add sour cream and carefully reheat (do not let boil). Adjust salt to taste. Add orange segments and garnish sauce with whole basil leaves.

➤ Serve with: Carrots, asparagus, poultry, fish, shrimp

Exotic | Hearty

Black Bean Sauce

SERVES 4:

➤ $1/2$ cup dry black beans

 Salt

 1 tomato

 1 onion

 1 clove garlic

 4 tsp olive oil

 1 cup vegetable stock

 1 pinch chili powder

 1 tbs freshly chopped parsley

🕐 Prep time: 30 minutes (+ soaking and cooking time for beans)

➤ Calories per serving: About 90

1 | Soak beans in water for 6 hours. Then, cover and simmer water-bean mixture for 1 hour or until softened over low heat. Salt lightly and stir occasionally. Drain beans when done and set aside.

2 | Rinse tomato and dice very finely. Peel onion and chop finely. Peel garlic and squeeze through a press.

3 | In a pot, heat oil and sauté onion for 1 minute over medium heat until translucent. Add garlic and cooked black beans and sauté for about 1 minute. Add half the vegetable stock, bring to a boil, and purée finely with a hand blender. Gradually add remaining stock while stirring until the sauce is the desired consistency. Season to taste with chili powder and salt as desired. Garnish with diced tomato and parsley.

➤ Serve with: Grilled meats, tortillas

Photo top: Orange-Basil Sauce   *Photo bottom:* Black Bean Sauce ➤

For Company | Fast

Sweet Mexican Chili Sauce

SERVES 4:

➤ 1 shallot

1 clove garlic

1 small zucchini (about ¼ lb)

¾ lb beefsteak tomatoes

4 tsp peanut oil

1 tbs freshly chopped cilantro

1 tbs vinegar

1 tbs honey

1 tbs fresh lime juice

1 pinch chili powder

Salt and pepper

🕐 Prep time: 20 minutes

➤ Calories per serving: About 80

1 | Peel shallot and dice finely. Peel garlic and squeeze through a press. Rinse zucchini and trim away ends. Rinse tomatoes, peel (cut a slit in tomatoes, soak in boiling water for 1 minute, and slip off peels), halve, and remove seeds. Cut zucchini and tomatoes into ¼-inch cubes. Combine all these ingredients in a pot and stir.

2 | Add peanut oil, chopped cilantro, vinegar, honey, fresh lime juice, chili powder, salt, and pepper to vegetables. Bring sauce briefly to a boil—ready to serve. Can be served hot or chilled.

➤ Serve with: Tortillas, grilled sausages, grilled vegetables

Spicy | For Company

Savory Mexican Chocolate Sauce

SERVES 4:

➤ 2 shallots

1 clove garlic

1 fresh red Fresno chile pepper

½ lb tomatoes

2 oz Mexican or semisweet chocolate

4 tsp peanut oil

⅓ cup sliced blanched almonds

1 pinch cinnamon

1 pinch aniseed

2 tbs vegetable stock

Salt and pepper

🕐 Prep time: 30 minutes

➤ Calories per serving: About 170

1 | Peel shallots and garlic. Rinse chile pepper and trim away stem. Finely chop all these ingredients. Rinse tomatoes and dice finely. Chop chocolate finely.

2 | Heat oil and sauté shallots, garlic, and chile pepper until translucent. Add almonds and cook for another minute. Add cinnamon, aniseed, and stock. Purée sauce with a hand blender. Add tomatoes and simmer for 3 minutes. Add chocolate and simmer for another 2 minutes. Season sauce with salt and pepper.

➤ Serve with: Tortillas, mixed grill, sautéed or roasted chicken or turkey breast

Photo top: Sweet Mexican Chili Sauce   *Photo bottom:* Savory Mexican Chocolate Sauce ➤

Cold Sauces and Pesto

Cold sauces are good with almost anything. They're quick and easy to throw together, and the preparation is generally uncomplicated. This makes them ideal both for every day and for parties.

Quick Recipes

Remoulade Sauce

SERVES 4:

➤ 1 green onion | 1 small pickling cucumber | 2 tsp capers | 1 tbs herbs (parsley, chives, chervil, tarragon) | 1 anchovy (optional) | $^1/_2$ cup light mayonnaise

1 | Rinse green onion, trim away unusable parts, and finely chop. Finely chop cucumber, capers, herbs, and, if desired, anchovy.

2 | Mix prepared ingredients with mayonnaise.

➤ Serve with: Steamed or grilled fish, chicken breast, roast beef, roasted or grilled vegetables

Cocktail Sauce

SERVES 4:

➤ $^1/_2$ cup light mayonnaise | 2 tbs ketchup | 2 tbs tomato paste | 1 pinch cayenne pepper | 2 tsp Hungarian sweet paprika | Salt and pepper

1 | Stir together mayonnaise, ketchup, and tomato paste until creamy.

2 | Season sauce to taste with cayenne, paprika, salt, and pepper.

➤ Serve with: Shrimp, grilled or fried fish, seafood, iceberg lettuce, or as a dip for raw vegetables

Traditional | Low-Fat

Buttermilk-Herb Sauce

SERVES 4:

- ➤ ³/4 cup fresh sprigs of green herbs (suggested combination: dill, chives, and/or tarragon)

  Greens from 2 green onions

  1 cup buttermilk

  2 tbs sour cream

  Salt and pepper

  1 pinch nutmeg

  Juice from 1 lime

- ⏱ Prep time: 20 minutes
- ➤ Calories per serving: About 30

1 | Rinse herbs and onion greens, pat dry, and chop all finely.

2 | Add buttermilk and purée mixture in a blender.

3 | Stir in sour cream and season sauce to taste with salt, pepper, nutmeg, and fresh lime juice.

- ➤ **Serve with:** Fish, cold roast beef, new potatoes, chilled sliced poultry

TIP You can also make this buttermilk-herb sauce with ²/3 cup yogurt (instead of buttermilk) and mix in ¹/3 cup crème fraîche or sour cream.

Can Prepare in Advance

Mayonnaise

MAKES ¹/2 CUP:

- ➤ 1 very fresh, whole egg

  1 tsp mustard

  1 splash vinegar

  1 pinch salt

  1 pinch sugar

  ¹/3 cup canola oil

  ¹/3 cup sour cream or firm yogurt (optional)

TIP **Light Curry Mayonnaise**
In an ungreased pan, carefully toast 1 tsp curry powder, add juice from 1 orange and set aside. Dice ¹/8 pineapple very finely. Stir all these ingredients into the light version of the traditional mayonnaise (recipe above). Season to taste with 1 tsp freshly grated ginger, salt, and pepper. Add 1 tbs finely chopped cilantro or Italian parsley. Serve curry mayonnaise with meat fondue, as a dip for raw vegetables, or with shrimp, cooked chicken, or hard-boiled eggs. It's also a great garnish for canapés.

- ⏱ Prep time: 15 minutes
- ➤ Calories per serving: About 75

1 | All ingredients should be at room temperature. In a tall container and using a hand blender, beat egg, mustard, vinegar, salt, sugar, and oil until foamy.

2 | If the mayonnaise is too thick, thin it with a little hot water. Let sauce stand for a moment.

3 | For a lighter mayonnaise, stir in sour cream or yogurt until smooth. Season to taste with salt.

- ➤ **Serve with:** Salads, vegetables, or use as a dip

Easy
Arugula Pesto

SERVES 8:

➤ 2 tsp pine nuts
1 clove garlic
2 cups arugula leaves
$1/3$ cup olive oil
$1^1/2$ oz freshly grated Parmesan
1 tsp grated lemon zest
Salt and pepper

🕘 Prep time: 15 minutes
➤ Calories per serving: About 100

1 | In an ungreased pan, toast pine nuts until golden over low heat. Peel garlic and squeeze through a press. Rinse arugula, and spin or pat dry.

2 | Using a hand blender, purée all ingredients finely while gradually adding olive oil in a stream. Season to taste with Parmesan, lemon zest, salt, and pepper.

➤ Serve with: Pasta, grilled dishes, mixed with balsamic vinegar dressing (page 51) to make a salad dressing, or as a dip for raw vegetables

Can Prepare in Advance
Tomato Pesto

SERVES 6:

➤ 1 tbs chopped blanched sliced almonds
$1/4$ lb sun-dried tomatoes
1 clove garlic
1 tbs freshly chopped oregano
1 tbs freshly chopped basil
$1/3$ cup olive oil
$1^1/2$ oz grated Parmesan
Salt and pepper

🕘 Prep time: 15 minutes
➤ Calories per serving: About 145

1 | In a dry pan, toast almonds until golden over medium heat. Reconstitute sun-dried tomatoes in boiling water, drain, and chop finely. Peel garlic and squeeze through a press.

2 | Using a hand blender, purée almonds, garlic, sun-dried tomatoes, oregano, and basil. Add oil. Season pesto to taste with Parmesan, salt, and pepper.

➤ Serve with: Pasta, vegetables, or as a spread

Mediterranean | Traditional
Pesto Genovese

SERVES 4:

➤ 2 tbs pine nuts
3 cloves garlic
3 bunches basil
$1/2$ cup olive oil
3 oz grated Parmesan
Salt and pepper

🕘 Prep time: 15 minutes
➤ Calories per serving: About 315

1 | In a dry pan, toast pine nuts until golden over low heat; let cool. Peel garlic. Remove basil leaves from stems, rinse, and pat dry. Chop these ingredients finely.

2 | Using a hand blender, purée all prepared ingredients while gradually adding oil in a thin stream until creamy.

3 | Add Parmesan and stir. Salt and pepper to taste.

➤ Serve with: Spaghetti (thin pesto with 3–4 tbs pasta water), grilled fish, lamb, zucchini, eggplant, broccoli

Dips and Dressings

What would fondue be without sauces, or raw vegetables without delicious dips, and grilled meats without marinades? You can never serve enough of these refreshing extras. Our spicy dressings help break up the monotony of everyday cuisine.

Quick Recipes

Tzatziki

MAKES 4 SERVINGS:

➤ $1/2$ cucumber | 1 clove garlic | $3/4$ cup yogurt and $3/4$ cup sour cream (or $1^1/3$ cups whole milk yogurt) | 2 tsp olive oil | 1 tsp minced dill | Salt and pepper

1 | Rinse cucumber, peel, remove seeds if desired and chop rest finely. Peel garlic, squeeze through a press, and mix with cucumber.

2 | Stir in yogurt, sour cream, and oil; season to taste with dill, salt, and pepper.

➤ Serve with: Gyros, souvlaki, or other Greek dishes; grilled pork, baked potatoes, toasted baguette slices, vegetables, as a spread for flatbread, or as a dip

Guacamole

SERVES 4:

➤ 1 clove garlic | 2 shallots | 2 tomatoes | 1 tbs chopped parsley | $1/4$ cup fresh lemon juice | $1/3$ tsp chili powder | Salt and pepper | 2 ripe avocados

1 | Peel garlic and shallots. Squeeze garlic through a press and dice shallots finely. Rinse tomatoes and dice. Combine with parsley, fresh lemon juice, chili powder, salt, and pepper.

2 | Peel avocadoes and remove pits. Mash half the avocado flesh with a fork, chop the other half and mix all ingredients together.

➤ Serve with: Grilled vegetables, smoked salmon, grilled fish, steak, or as a dip for tortilla chips or raw vegetable sticks (such as jicama and cucumber)

43

Can Prepare in Advance

Apricot Yogurt Dip

SERVES 4:

- 5 apricots

  2 tsp honey

  Juice from $1^1/_2$ lemons

  1 cup firm yogurt

  2 tbs mayonnaise

  2 tsp prepared horseradish (from a jar)

  Salt and pepper

- Prep time: 15 minutes
- Calories per serving: About 130

1 | Rinse apricots and remove pits. Dice 3 apricots finely and purée remaining 2 with honey and fresh lemon juice.

2 | Combine yogurt, mayonnaise, and horseradish until creamy. Carefully fold in diced apricots and puréed apricot mixture. Season dip with salt and pepper.

- **Serve with: Shrimp, poultry, grilled foods, or as a dip for raw vegetables**

Low-Fat

Vegetable Salsa

SERVES 4:

- 1 red bell pepper

  2 tomatoes

  1 small zucchini ($1/_4$ lb)

  1 small red onion

  1 clove garlic

  1–2 lemons

  1 tbs olive oil (optional)

  1 tbs freshly chopped cilantro or parsley

  Salt and pepper

- Prep time: 20 minutes (+ 30 minutes marinating time)
- Calories per serving: About 65

1 | Rinse bell pepper, tomatoes, and zucchini. Cut bell pepper, tomatoes, and zucchini into $1/_4$-inch cubes. Peel onion and garlic and chop both very finely.

2 | Squeeze juice from lemon and mix with chopped ingredients. Add olive oil if desired. Stir in cilantro or parsley, salt, and pepper and marinate for 30 minutes.

- **Serve with: Pasta, grilled meat, fish**

Fast | For a Buffet

Radish-Herb Dip

SERVES 4:

- 1 piece of cucumber ($1/_4$ lb)

  1 clove garlic

  1 tbs fresh lemon juice

  Salt and pepper

  1 cup low-fat sour cream

  1 tbs olive oil

  1 cup radishes

  $1/_2$ red bell pepper

  1 bunch chives

  $1/_2$ cup parsley sprigs

- Prep time: 20 minutes
- Calories per serving: About 80

1 | Peel cucumber, halve lengthwise, and remove seeds with a spoon tip. Peel garlic. Purée these together with fresh lemon juice, salt, and pepper. Blend with sour cream and olive oil until creamy.

2 | Rinse radishes, bell pepper, chives, and parsley. Grate radishes, dice usable parts of bell pepper, and mince chives and parsley. Add these to sour cream mixture. Stir; salt and pepper to taste.

- **Serve with: Raw vegetables, new potatoes**

Spicy | Fast

Creole Marinade

SERVES 6:

- ➤ $^1/_4$ lb papaya
  $^1/_4$ lb cucumbers
  1 large ripe tomato
  4 sprigs cilantro
  1 piece fresh ginger
  ($^1/_2$-inch section)
  $^1/_4$ cup coconut milk
  1 tbs garlic chile oil
  Juice of 2 limes
  Salt and pepper

- 🕒 Prep time: 15 minutes
- ➤ Calories per serving:
  About 35

1 | Rinse papaya, cucumbers, tomato, and cilantro. Remove seeds from papaya and dice finely with cucumber and tomato. Chop cilantro; grate ginger.

2 | Combine above with remaining ingredients. Salt and pepper to taste; let stand for 30 minutes.

- ➤ Serve with: as a marinade for carpaccio, meats, vegetables to be grilled; or as a dressing for salad or seafood cocktail

Asian | Low-Fat

Fig Chutney

SERVES 4:

- ➤ 4 fresh figs
  1 onion
  1 piece fresh ginger
  ($^1/_2$-inch section)
  1 tbs honey
  1 tbs raspberry vinegar
  2 tbs fresh lime juice
  1 pinch chili powder
  Salt and pepper

- 🕒 Prep time: 15 minutes
- ➤ Calories per serving:
  About 45

1 | Rinse figs and cut into $^1/_4$-inch cubes. Peel onion and dice finely. Peel ginger and grate finely.

2 | In a pot, heat honey over medium heat. As soon as it turns golden, cook onion in it until translucent. Add figs and ginger. Add vinegar and fresh lime juice; simmer for 1 minute. Season to taste with chili powder, salt, and pepper.

- ➤ Serve with: Poultry, rabbit, pâté, rice dishes

Asian | For Company

Apricot Chutney

SERVES 4:

- ➤ $^3/_4$ lb apricots
  2 small onions
  2 tsp butter
  $^1/_2$ tsp ground allspice
  1 tbs honey
  1 pinch ground coriander
  1 pinch ground cumin
  Salt and pepper
  2 tbs freshly chopped mint

- 🕒 Prep time: 30 minutes
- ➤ Calories per serving:
  About 70

1 | Rinse apricots and remove pits. Peel onions. Dice both ingredients finely.

2 | Heat butter and sauté onions and apricots for 8 minutes.

3 | Season with allspice, honey, coriander, and cumin. Stir in $^1/_3$ cup water, cover, and simmer over low heat for about 15 minutes. Season to taste with salt and pepper; stir in mint.

- ➤ Serve with: Rice dishes, game, poultry

Mediterranean | For Company

Salsa Verde

SERVES 4:

- 1 green bell pepper
  2 cups Italian parsley sprigs
  1 small onion
  1 clove garlic
  3 anchovy fillets
  1 tbs capers
  $1^1/_2$ tbs olive oil
  2 tbs fresh lemon juice
  Salt and pepper

⏱ Prep time: 15 minutes
- Calories per serving: About 80

1 | Rinse bell pepper. Rinse parsley and pat dry. Peel onion and garlic. Finely dice usable parts of these ingredients. Chop anchovies.

2 | Using a hand blender, purée above with capers, olive oil, and fresh lemon juice to produce a creamy paste. Season to taste with salt and pepper. Serve in a bell pepper half if desired.

- Serve with: Poached meats, eggplant, zucchini

Fast | For a Buffet

Zucchini-Herb Relish

SERVES 4:

- 1 zucchini ($^1/_2$ lb)
  4 sprigs fresh tarragon
  4 sprigs fresh basil
  3 mint leaves
  $^2/_3$ cup preserving sugar (specialty store)
  $^1/_2$ tsp black pepper
  3 tbs raspberry vinegar
  1 piece fresh ginger ($^1/_2$-inch section)
  Salt

⏱ Prep time: 15 minutes
  Calories per serving: About 165

1 | Rinse zucchini, tarragon, basil, and mint; mince all. Combine zucchini, preserving sugar, pepper, vinegar, and ginger; boil.

2 | Add tarragon, basil, and mint; simmer for 4 minutes. Salt to taste. While hot, pour into screw-top jars and seal. Relish keeps for 1 week refrigerated.

- Serve with: Stir-fries, cold cooked poultry

Can Prepare in Advance

Cucumber Relish

SERVES 4:

- 2 shallots
  1 clove garlic
  $^1/_2$ cucumber
  $^1/_3$ lb pumpkin
  2 tbs white wine vinegar
  $^1/_2$ tsp freshly chopped tarragon or chives
  1 tbs honey
  Salt and pepper

⏱ Prep time: 30 minutes (+ 30 minutes marinating time)
- Calories per serving: About 35

1 | Peel shallots and dice very finely. Peel garlic and mince. Rinse cucumber, remove seeds from cucumber and pumpkin, and cut both into $^1/_4$-inch cubes. In a bowl, combine shallots, garlic, cucumber, and pumpkin.

2 | Stir in vinegar, tarragon or chives, honey, salt, and pepper. Marinate relish for 30 minutes.

- Serve with: Grilled fish, asparagus, roasted or grilled bell peppers

Can Prepare in Advance

Balsamic Vinegar Dressing

SERVES 4:

- ➤ 4 tbs balsamic vinegar
- 2 tbs vegetable stock
- $1/2$ tsp prepared mustard
- $1^1/2$ tbs olive oil
- 1 small clove garlic
- 1 tsp freshly chopped thyme
- Salt and pepper

⊙ Prep time: 10 minutes

- ➤ Calories per serving: About 35

1 | Combine vinegar, stock, and mustard. Whisk in oil.

2 | Peel garlic, squeeze through a press, and add. Add thyme; salt and pepper to taste.

- ➤ **Serve with: Arugula salad, green salads, raw vegetables, stir-fried or sautéed vegetables**

TIP For fast cooking, prepare 3 to 4 times the recipe and keep in screw-top jars refrigerated (keeps for a week or two).

Fast | Can Prepare in Advance

Herb Dressing

SERVES 4:

- ➤ 2 tbs fresh lime juice
- 2 tsp prepared mustard
- $1/4$ cup vegetable stock
- 2 tbs oil
- 2 tbs freshly chopped herbs (parsley, basil, chives)
- Salt and pepper

⊙ Prep time: 10 minutes

- ➤ Calories per serving: About 50

1 | Combine fresh lime juice, mustard, and stock. Gradually whisk in oil.

2 | Stir in chopped herbs; season dressing to taste with salt and pepper.

- ➤ **Serve with: Green salads, as a marinade for vegetable or fish carpaccios, or as a dip for raw vegetables**

TIP To be ready to entertain at short notice, prepare larger quantities of the basic dressing and always add the herbs fresh. This dressing keeps for 1 week in the refrigerator.

Fast | For Company

Apple-Walnut Oil Dressing

SERVES 4:

- ➤ 1 shallot
- $1/2$ apple
- 2 tsp oil
- 1 tsp walnut oil
- 3 tbs wine vinegar
- 1 tsp honey
- 1 tsp prepared mustard
- $1/3$ cup vegetable stock
- 2 tbs freshly chopped parsley
- Salt and pepper

⊙ Prep time: 10 minutes

- ➤ Calories per serving: About 55

1 | Peel shallot and dice finely. Rinse apple, remove core, and dice rest very finely.

2 | Combine oils, vinegar, honey, mustard, vegetable stock, parsley, salt, and pepper; whisk. Stir in apple and shallot.

- ➤ **Serve with: Salad, raw vegetables, frisée salad, radicchio, carrots**

◄ *Photo left:* **Balsamic Vinegar Dressing**   *Photo top:* **Herb Dressing**   *Photo right:* **Apple-Walnut Oil Dressing**

Sweet Sauces

If you love to end meals with an unforgettable finale, experiment with dessert sauces! Whether you choose a semisweet chocolate sauce, a creamy vanilla sauce, or a fresh fruit sauce, these deliciously sweet sauces will enhance the flavor of any dessert.

Quick Recipes

Apricot Sauce

SERVES 4:

➤ $1/2$ lb apricots | $1/2$ cup orange juice |
$2 1/2$ tbs sugar | $1/2$ tsp vanilla

1 | Rinse apricots, cut in half, remove pits, and chop finely.

2 | Using a hand blender, purée apricots with orange juice. Sweeten with sugar and stir in vanilla.

➤ **Serve with: Ice cream, vanilla pudding, panna cotta, crème brûlée**

Raspberry Sauce

SERVES 4:

➤ 2 tbs sugar | $3/4$ lb raspberries | 1 tbs
sugar | $1/2$ tsp vanilla | 1 tsp fresh
lemon juice

1 | Heat sugar and 2 tbs water. Pour into a tall container with raspberries and purée with a hand blender.

2 | Season to taste with sugar, vanilla, and fresh lemon juice.

➤ **Serve with: Ice cream, panna cotta, crème brûlée, chocolate volcano cake**

53

Easy

Orange Sauce

SERVES 4:

➤ **2 oranges**
3 tbs sugar
$1/3$ tsp freshly grated ginger
1 tsp freshly chopped mint

🕐 Prep time: 20 minutes
➤ Calories per serving:
About 55

1 | Squeeze juice from 1 orange. Dice the fruit of second orange finely (after peeling).

2 | Bring juice to a boil with sugar and ginger. Add diced orange and bring to a boil again, then remove from heat and let cool. Serve sprinkled with mint. You can serve this sauce warm or cold.

➤ **Serve with: Pancakes, crêpes, ice cream, fruit salads, strawberries, creamy desserts**

For Company | Traditional

Mocha Sauce

SERVES 4:

➤ **$2 1/2$ oz semi-sweet chocolate**
$1/3$ cup extra-strong coffee
$1/4$ cup whole milk
$1/4$ cup cream
3 tbs sugar

🕐 Prep time: 15 minutes
➤ Calories per serving:
About 175

1 | Chop chocolate finely and bring to a boil with coffee, milk, and cream while stirring or whisking constantly until the chocolate has dissolved.

2 | Sweeten with sugar and remove from heat. Can be served hot or cold.

➤ **Serve with: Pancakes, ice cream, bananas, berries, angel food cake, chocolate cake, pound cake**

TIP Replace the coffee with more cream and flavor it with a little vanilla bean pulp or, for adults, a little Cognac, Armagnac or other spirit.

Fast | Easy

Strawberry-Rhubarb Sauce

SERVES 4:

➤ **$1/4$ lb rhubarb**
2 tbs sugar
$1/2$ tsp vanilla
1 lb strawberries

🕐 Prep time: 20 minutes
➤ Calories per serving:
About 45

1 | Rinse rhubarb, peel, and cut into $1/4$-inch cubes. In a pot, heat sugar and 1 tbs water. Add rhubarb. Bring to a boil, then remove from heat. Mix in vanilla and let cool.

2 | In the meantime, rinse strawberries and remove stems. Chop finely and purée with a hand blender or in a blender or food processor.

3 | Add puréed strawberries to rhubarb mixture and sweeten with more sugar to taste.

➤ **Serve with: English puddings, vanilla pudding, panna cotta, crème brûlée, ice cream, pound cake, angel food cake, shortcake**

Can Prepare in Advance
Rosemary-Plum Sauce

SERVES 4:

- ¾ lb plums
  3 tbs honey
  ½ tsp freshly minced rosemary
  1 tbs sugar
  ½ tsp vanilla
  1 tbs fresh lemon juice
  1 pinch cinnamon

🕙 Prep time: 30 minutes
- Calories per serving: About 185

1 | Rinse plums, cut in half, and remove pits. Dice.

2 | In a pot, caramelize 2 tbs honey over medium heat until golden. Stir in plums, rosemary, sugar, and vanilla; simmer for about 2 minutes or until plums are soft. Add fresh lemon juice, remove from heat, and purée using a hand blender. Put through a strainer and season to taste with honey and cinnamon.

- **Serve with: pancakes, ice cream, rice pudding, pound cake**

Fast | For Company
Grapefruit-Caramel Sauce

SERVES 4:

- 4 pink grapefruit
  ½ cup orange juice
  ¼ cup sugar
  4 tsp butter
  1 tbs sugar
  ½ tsp vanilla
  1 pinch cinnamon

🕙 Prep time: 15 minutes
- Calories per serving: About 130

1 | Juice 1 grapefruit (set aside). Cut peels from other grapefruit (including white part) and cut segments out of the inside membrane. Combine segments with orange juice; set aside.

2 | In a pan, caramelize sugar over medium heat until golden. Add grapefruit-orange juice mixture; cook for 1 minute. Add reserved grapefruit juice. Stir in butter; don't let sauce boil again. Season to taste with remaining sugar, vanilla, and cinnamon.

- **Serve with: Ice cream, crêpes, any creamy dessert**

Traditional | Easy
Vanilla Sauce

SERVES 4:

- 1⅔ cups milk
  1 heaping tbs cornstarch
  ¼ cup sugar
  1 egg yolk
  1 vanilla bean

🕙 Prep time: 10 minutes
- Calories per serving: About 145

1 | Stir together ¼ cup of the milk, cornstarch, sugar, and egg yolk.

2 | Slit open vanilla bean lengthwise and remove pulp. In a pot, slowly heat remaining milk, vanilla pulp, and vanilla bean over medium heat and bring to a boil. Add egg yolk mixture while stirring constantly until the sauce takes on a creamy consistency. Don't let it boil again or it will curdle (but do let it heat up slightly after you add the egg yolk mixture). Remove vanilla bean and serve.

- **Serve with: Ice cream, chocolate pudding, berries, apple strudel, chocolate cake**

Which Sauce Goes with What?

Sauce	Page	With meat, poultry, game	With fish	With vegetables and/or potatoes	With pasta	With rice	With salads	With desserts
Apple-Walnut Oil Dressing	51			X			X	
Apricot Chutney	47	X				X		
Apricot Sauce	53							X
Apricot Yogurt Dip	45	X	X				X	
Arugula Pesto	41	X			X		X	
Asian Vegetable Sauce	24	X	X		X	X		
Balsamic Vinegar Dressing	51			X			X	
Béchamel Sauce	12		X	X				
Bell Pepper Sauce	11			X	X	X		
Black Bean Sauce	32	X						
Buttermilk-Herb Sauce	38	X	X	X				
Cheese Topping	12		X	X	X			
Clam Sauce	24		X	X	X	X		
Cocktail Sauce	37		X				X	
Cranberry-Chestnut Sauce	27	X		X				
Creole Marinade	47	X	X				X	
Cucumber Relish	49		X	X				
Curry Leek Sauce	21	X	X	X	X	X		
Fig Chutney	47	X				X		
Grapefruit-Caramel Sauce	57							X
Ground Meat Sauce	15			X	X	X		
Guacamole	43	X	X	X			X	
Herb Dressing	51		X				X	
Hollandaise Sauce	17	X	X	X				
Horseradish Sauce	19	X	X	X				
Mayonnaise	38						X	
Mexican Chocolate Sauce	34	X						

Sauce	Page	With meat, poultry, game	With fish	With vegetables and/or potatoes	With pasta	With rice	With salads	With desserts
Mocha Sauce	55							X
Mushroom Sauce	19	X		X	X			
Onion-Marjoram Sauce	27	X		X				
Orange Sauce	55							X
Orange-Basil Sauce	32	X	X	X				
Parmesan Sauce	15	X		X	X			
Passion Fruit Sauce	30	X	X					
Pesto Genovese	41	X	X	X	X			
Prosecco Sauce	27	X	X					
Rabbit Sauce with Olives	29		X	X				
Radish-Herb Dip	45			X			X	
Raspberry Sauce	53							X
Remoulade Sauce	37	X	X					
Rosemary-Plum Sauce	57							X
Salsa Verde	49	X		X				
Shallot and Red Wine Sauce	19	X	X					
Strawberry-Rhubarb Sauce	55							X
Sweet-and-Sour Sauce	15	X	X			X		
Sweet Mexican Chile Sauce	34	X						
Tomato-Eggplant Sauce	22		X	X	X	X		
Tomato Pesto	41	X		X	X		X	
Tomato Sauce	21	X	X	X	X	X		
Tomato Sauce with Capers and Tuna	22	X	X	X	X	X		
Tzatziki	43	X		X			X	
Vanilla Sauce	57							X
Vegetable Salsa	45	X	X		X			
Vegetable Sauce	11	X		X	X	X		
Walnut Sauce	30	X	X		X			
Zucchini-Herb Relish	49	X						

ABBREVIATIONS

lb = pound
oz = ounce
tsp = teaspoon
tbs = tablespoon

The Author

Elisabeth Döpp has enjoyed a lengthy career working for publishing houses and as a health trainer for nutrition, specializing in vegetarian and healthful cuisines.
Christian Willrich of Alsace has been working as a chef in fine dining restaurants since 1980. His focus is organic cuisine.
Jörn Rebbe trained as a chef in a Japanese hotel. As a chef de cuisine, he specializes in Japanese and Chinese foods.

The Photographer

Kai Mewes is an independent food photographer in Munich who works for publishers and in advertising. His studio and test kitchen are located near Munich's Viktualienmarkt. His appetizing photos reflect his dedication to combining photography and culinary pleasure. Food styling is the work of Akos Neuberger.

Photo Credits

FoodPhotographie Eising, Martina Görlach: cover photo
Stockfood: page 6
All others: Kai Mewes

Published originally under the title Saucen und Dips: zum Reinlegen gut © 2002 Gräfe und Unzer Verlag GmbH, Munich. English translation for the U.S. market © 2003, Silverback Books, Inc.

Translation: Christie Tam
American food editor: Kelsey Lane
Managing editor: Birgit Rademacker
Editor: Stefanie Poziombka
Readers: Lynda Zuber Sassi, Bettina Bartz and Mischa Gallé
Recipe testing: Karl Broich Catering-Company, Düsseldorf
Layout, typography, and cover design: Independent Medien-Design, Munich
Production: Patty Holden and Maike Harmeier
Typesetting: Design-Typo-Print GmbH, Ismaning
Reproduction, printing and binding: China

ISBN 1-930603-62-2

Enjoy Other Quick & Easy Books

Cooking for One
Christina Kempe

Cocktails & Mixed Drinks
Tanja Dusy & Alessandra Redies

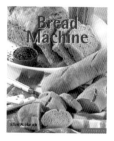

Bread Machine
Ellen A. Hatch

Cooking for Children
Cramm

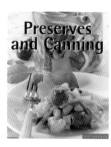

Preserves and Canning

Irresistible Fondue
Angelika Illies

Cooking for Two
Cornelia Adam

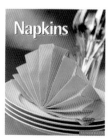

Napkins

Fast Italian
Margit Proebst

Sushi
Andreas Fürtmayr

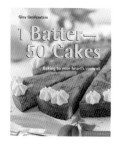

1 Batter—50 Cakes
Gina Greifenstein

Baking to your heart's content

Cooking in Clay
Hearty Recipes with Great Flavor
Erika Casparek-Türkkan

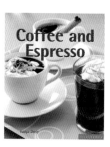

Coffee and Espresso
Tanja Dusy

Grilling
Antje Gruener

Sauces and Dips

Soups
Classic to Contemporary
Sebastian Dickhaut

Raclette
New Recipes with Cheese Primer and Party Dips
Claudia Schmidt

Antipasti and Tapas
Mediterranean Appetizers
Cornelia Schinharl

1 Pan—50 Muffins

Salads
Cornelia Adam

Sandwiches

Fondue
Melise Szwillus

Cheese, vegetable, broth kinds of meat—everyone's right at the table with these menus

Christmas Cookies

ROASTING LIKE A PRO

➤ When roasting or sautéing vegetables for a sauce, turn up the heat and don't be too timid. The color of the roasted vegetables tells you what color your sauce will be. If the vegetables you used were too dark, put the sauce through a strainer to catch any over-browned bits.

Success with Sauces and Dips

NO COLD ENCOUNTERS

➤ Hot sauces, and especially gravies, should always be transferred to a prewarmed gravy boat or small bowl. This will keep them hot longer and they won't form an unappetizing skin on top. Use a sterno burner and/or chafing dish set-up to keep your hot sauces hot at the table.

DO NOT BOIL

➤ Many sauces are sensitive to high heat. Some sauces will curdle, especially those containing egg, sour cream, yogurt, or other low-fat dairy products. When cream curdles, the sauce looks unappetizing and separates so keep an eye on your sauce and remove it from the heat when it's hot but before it boils.

FRESH IS BEST

➤ Even if many of our sauces can be prepared in advance, you should always try to prepare them fresh if possible. Obviously this is true of hot sauces that lose some of their flavor when reheated, but it also applies to cold sauces, dressings, and dips, which are best when freshly mixed.